Many Ways to Travel

Maneras de viajar

comment se déplacer

多種方式的旅遊

text by Jocelyn Graeme
photos by Ruth Fahlman, May Henderson, and Michael Johnson

Addison-Wesley Publishers Limited
Don Mills, Ontario • Reading, Massachusetts
Menlo Park, California • New York
Wokingham, England • Amsterdam • Bonn
Sydney • Singapore • Tokyo • Madrid • San Juan

728816

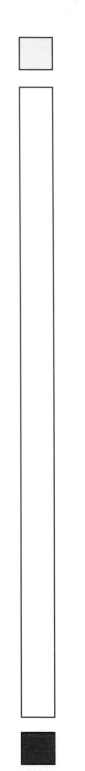

We can travel many ways.

Comment se déplacer.

Podemos viajar de muchas maneras.

我們有多種的旅遊方式。

We can snuggle up close in a backpack or sling.

Nous pouvons être serrés dans un porte-bébé en avant ou en arrière.

Podemos cobijarnos en una mochila o en un cabestrillo.

我們可以蜷伏在後包或皮背帶。

We can ride on the back of a donkey or horse.

Nous pouvons monter à dos d'âne ou à cheval.

Podemos viajar sobre el lomo de una mula o un caballo.

我們可以騎在驢子或馬的背上。

We can pedal a bike that has two wheels or three.

Nous pouvons rouler à bicyclette ou en tricycle.

Podemos pedalear una bicicleta o un triciclo.

我們可以踏在有二輪或三輪的
脚踏車。

We can wheel safely along in a stroller or wheelchair.

Nous pouvons nous promener en poussette ou en chaise roulante.

Podemos andar seguros en un cochecito o en una silla de ruedas.

我們可以很安全的在有輪子的兒童推車或輪椅上轉動。

We can ride down the road in a bus or a car.

Nous pouvons circuler sur la route en autobus ou en automobile.

Podemos viajar por la calle en un autobús o en un automóvil.

我們可以乘坐巴士或汽車。

We can roll down the rails in a train or a trolley.

Nous pouvons filer sur des rails à bord d'un train ou d'un tramway.

Podemos deslizarnos por los rieles en un tren o en un trolebús.

我們可以滑行在火車或吊運車上。

We can float on the waves in a seabus or boat.

Nous pouvons naviguer en traversier ou en bateau.

Podemos flotar sobre las olas en un transbordador o en una lancha.

我們可以飄浮在渡海小輪或小船裏。

We can take off and land in a helicopter or airplane.

Nous pouvons décoller et atterrir à bord d'un hélicoptère ou d'un avion.

Podemos despegar y aterrizar en un helicóptero o en un avión.

我們可以起飛在直升機或客機上。

We can slide over snow in a sled or snowmobile.

Nous pouvons glisser sur la neige à bord d'un traîneau ou d'une motoneige.

Podemos deslizarnos sobre la nieve en un trineo o en un esquidú.

我們可以用雪橇或雪上摩托車滑雪。

And we can travel many ways when we pretend.

Avec un peu d'imagination nous pouvons trouver bien des façons de nous déplacer.

Y podemos viajar de muchas maneras cuando pretendemos.

讓我們偽裝多種旅行工具的遊戲。

Sponsoring Editor: Beth Bruder

Designer: Pamela Kinney

Editor: Lauren E. Wolk

Translators
Spanish: Edith Stagni
Brenda Cortes

French: Katherine Stauble
Martine Brassard

Chinese: Mei-lin Cheung
Sew Pim Lim
Hsiao Chiang

Sponsor: Early Childhood Multicultural Services
Early Childhood Multicultural Services gratefully acknowledges the support and financial assistance of the Multiculturalism Directorate, Secretary of State, Canada; the Cabinet Committee on Cultural Heritage, Province of British Columbia; and the Preschool ESL Committee (PRESL), Vancouver.

Canadian Cataloguing in Publication Data

Graeme, Jocelyn, 1958–
Many ways to travel

(Hand in hand)
Text in English, Chinese, French, Spanish.
ISBN 0-201-54650-7 (set). – ISBN 0-201-54657-4 (School Edition)
ISBN 0-201-54743-0 (Trade Edition)

1. Transportation – Juvenile literature.
2. Vehicles – Juvenile literature. I. Fahlman,
Ruth, 1954–   . II. Henderson, May. III. Title.
IV. Series: Hand in hand (Don Mills, Ont.).

HE152.G73 1990   388   C90-094218-5

ISBN 0-201-54657-4 (School Edition)   **ISBN 0-201-54743-0** (Trade Edition)

Printed in Canada

A B C D E F – ALG – 95 94 93 92 91 90